I0606348

Toucan

by Grace Hansen

Abdo Kids Jumbo is an Imprint of Abdo Kids
abdobooks.com

abdobooks.com

Published by Abdo Kids, a division of ABDO, P.O. Box 398166, Minneapolis, Minnesota 55439.

Printed in the United States of America, North Mankato, Minnesota.

052022

092022

Photo Credits: Getty Images, Minden Pictures, Shutterstock

Production Contributors: Teddy Borth, Jennie Forsberg, Grace Hansen
Design Contributors: Candice Keimig, Victoria Bates

Library of Congress Control Number: 2021950556

Publisher's Cataloging-in-Publication Data

Names: Hansen, Grace, author.

Title: Toucan / by Grace Hansen.

Description: Minneapolis, Minnesota : Abdo Kids, 2023 | Series: South American animals | Includes online resources and index.

Identifiers: ISBN 9781098261863 (lib. bdg.) | ISBN 9781098262709 (ebook) | ISBN 9781098263126 (Read-to-Me ebook)

Subjects: LCSH: Toucans--Juvenile literature. | Birds--Juvenile literature. | South America--Juvenile literature. | Rain forest animals--Juvenile literature. | Zoology--Juvenile literature.

Classification: DDC 598.7--dc23

Table of Contents

South America

South America is filled with lovely landscapes, from rain forests to mountain ranges. Because of these special places, a **diverse** group of animals live on the **continent**. Toucans are just some of these animals.

Keel-billed toucan
North America
Europe
Asia
Africa
South America

Toucans

Toucans live throughout southern Mexico and Central and South America. There are around 35 different toucan **species**.

Plate-billed
mountain toucan

The largest and best-known species is the toco toucan. It lives in South America's tropical rain forests.

Toco toucans can grow to be nearly 2 pounds (0.9 kg). They are about 25 inches (63.5 cm) long.

Toco toucans have shiny black feathers. White feathers cover their throats. Their eyes are surrounded by blue and yellow rings of bare skin.

Food

Toucans are best known for their large and colorful beaks. A toucan's beak is surprisingly light for its size. The bird uses its beak to reach, pluck, and peel fruit.

Toucans eat other things too. They like to hunt insects, small reptiles, and frogs. They will also find and eat the eggs of other birds.

Baby Toucans

Toucans often live in groups. Males and females **mate** in spring. Females lay their eggs in tree **cavities**. They lay up to 5 shiny eggs.

Collared aracari toucan

Both parents work to keep the eggs warm. The eggs hatch after about 20 days. The parents protect and care for their chicks. After about 8 weeks, the chicks are ready to leave the nest.

More Facts

- Toucans are more likely to hop from branch to branch rather than fly.
- Toucans are very noisy birds. They make loud croaking and barking noises.
- There are four **species** of mountain toucan. They all live in the forests of the Andes Mountains. They make very short, seasonal **migrations** up and down the mountains in search of food.

Glossary

cavity – a hollow place or hole.

continent – one of the earth's seven major areas of land. The continents are Africa, Antarctica, Asia, Australia, Europe, North America, and South America.

diverse – of different kinds or sorts.

mate – to come together to have young.

migration – the act of migrating. To migrate is to move from one place to another, usually to find food and/or have young.

species – a group of living things that look alike and can have young together.

tropical – having a climate in which there is no frost and where plants can grow all year long.

Index